KEEP GOING!

HOW NOT TO GIVE UP ON YOUR DREAMS WHEN IT'S HARD.

ANNA ENNIS

CONTENTS

ISBN: 978-1-950621-19-4 (ebook)

ISBN: 978-1-950621-18-7 (paperback)

DEDICATION

I dedicate this book to the girls in my life.

Mom, for believing in me on those days, I wanted to give up on the dream I wished for as a girl.

My daughters, who have been my biggest life teachers, cheerleaders, and at times a bit too honest.

My best friend and business partner who pushed me to actually finish this even when I tried to get out of it a million times.

AND ONE DAY SHE
DISCOVERED THAT
SHE WAS FIERCE,
AND STRONG,
AND FULL OF
FIRE,
AND THAT NOT
EVEN SHE COULD
HOLD HERSELF
BACK
BECAUSE HER
PASSION BURNED
BRIGHTER THAN
HER FEARS.

- Mark Anthony

ACKNOWLEDGMENTS

I would be remiss if I didn't say thank you to some extraordinary people in my life who believed in me when I questioned whether "I could":

JASON, I love you. You drive me crazy. You make me laugh. You have made my life amazing and full of color. You have put up with my shenanigans and told me to jump off the bridge; I don't know how many times. Thank you. Because of you, I feel even stronger, smarter, and more spontaneous. Well, no… spontaneous is something I'm always going to have to work on.

RICH, the first dude who said, "Hell yes" to just about every wild idea I had when we were younger. The one who defended any bad choice I made as "it was all them, not you." My best buddy. My brother. Thank you for being a badass Marine who never stops being one step better than you were the day before.

LARRY, MICHELLE, FRANK, & DEBBIE, I promised myself 18 years ago when I set the goal to write books that I would write on the first page of my first book, my deepest gratitude to you all. When I was 21 sitting inside a vision board workshop that our company had put on (when vision boards were not a thing yet), I decided to be an author. I placed a picture of a person who then was an author, speaker, and changed lives for a living as my goal. For someone that spells terribly, speaks in slang most of the time, and says dude way too much, my goal felt like a stretch but here we are!

Thank you for opening my eyes for 17 years of what's possible.

Here is the first of many to come.

CHAPTER 1

THE "C" WORD

As humans, we love our comfort. We are on autopilot, thinking a good life is a comfortable life.

— *Anna Ennis*

1. **THE "C" WORD**

WHEN YOU HAVE BEEN AT SOMETHING FOR A LONG TIME, it's been said change can feel darn near impossible. I know for me, there were times achieving my dreams felt a million miles away.

I think if you're anything like me, you can relate. There are so many times where I desperately wanted to make changes in myself, my life and would start and stop. Then feel like crap about myself and feel even more hopeless that I couldn't make the big dreams in my heart and head turn into reality.

Exercise hurts. Comfort food feels oh so good. Learning a new skill feels like it takes way too much time and effort. Planning a vacation with kids is just way too much work.

It's easier to stay where we are and do what we usually do.

As humans, we love our comfort. Take a look at our society. We have a drive-through for everything, including our groceries. We can have anything and everything delivered to our house at any moment of the day. We choose just about anything to make our lives easier.

It's almost as though we are on autopilot, thinking a good life is a comfortable life.

Then something happens. Life happens. You wake up and realize you've hated your job for a long time. You remember what you wanted to do with your life. You look around at what you're doing, how you're living, and what you're feeling feels way off track. Stuck. Hamster wheel-ish. You start thinking about what you had imagined your life would be like. What if you got clear on what you really wanted. What if you started making that happen. Maybe you start feeling a little bit excited. Hope starts moving through your body, along with the excitement that things can change. You start thinking about what you would feel like healthier. You would have so much more energy. You might feel excited about your clothes simply because you feel good in your skin. You think to yourself, Yeah! I can do this.

I'm gonna start making some changes. I can't stand this place that I'm in anymore! I am going to make it happen. You make a list of things you might need to do differently to start changing the trajectory of where your life is going. Let's say, for the sake of argument, the issue lies in your career path.

You look at your current schedule; you see that you have an extra hour in the morning and an extra hour in the evening. You could start working on your own consulting business. The excitement continues to rise, and you feel the hope of a better feeling life continue to increase inside of you. Yes! This is very exciting! You've been exhausted, so it would be best if you had a little more energy, too. You decide to start eating healthier than you have been. Declarations are made and scheduled, and a plan is laid out: From 6 am to 7 AM, I will work on my new business. And from 5 pm to 6 pm I'm going to work on my new business. I am going to eat a healthy lunch and a healthy dinner. Yes! I am changing my life! I am going to start this on Monday!

Monday morning comes, and you realize you went to bed a little too late Sunday night. Further, you ate a meal like it was your last supper because the next day, you were cutting out all the crap. The late-night resulted in you waking up to an alarm that felt like it was going off in the middle of the night. It was going off at 5:30 AM because you planned to start working on your new business at 6 am. Instead, you hit snooze several times. Ugh. You just can't get out of bed. Finally, rolling out of bed at about 6:30 am, feeling exhausted as usual. You get some coffee to wake up a little before you start working on your new business. By the time you sit down at your computer, it's 6:55 am. Great. I've got five minutes to work on my new business. Five minutes isn't even long enough for me to brush my teeth, let alone work on my new company. I guess I'll start this later tonight in the second hour I blocked out.

Lunch comes, and you realize you're frustrated about your rough start to your game plan, and you missed breakfast, so you're starving. Healthy food doesn't look like it's going to touch your hunger with a 10-foot pole. Plus, you're feeling down because it's Monday, and you already have feelings of discouragement and overwhelm. You remember all the times you've wanted to make a change and how many times you haven't been able to. Instead of eating healthy, you have what you would typically have and decide you'll try to make some changes in the future when you don't feel so frustrated and overwhelmed with everything. The hamster wheel continues to roll, and off you go.

You know the drill. We all know the drill. I know the drill very well, and that's why I'm so passionate about doing what it takes to make a lasting change--because I have been there feeling so stuck and beyond devastated.

You see where I'm going with this because this has happened to all of us at some point. We declare our desperate and sincere desire for our lives to be different. We get excited about the prospect of having a better feeling life. We make a plan. We go to execute the plan. We feel uncomfortable with the changes...and we downshift back into the gear we are used to driving in. Slowing down wouldn't be so bad, except now we have acquired more proof to rub in our own faces that we are stuck. Change is too hard. If we're really on one, which most of us are from time to time, we heap on the shame. We say things like I am such a failure. Or I am weak. Or something is wrong with me. We often can't acknowledge that we are shaming ourselves, so we attempt to sidestep those horrible feelings and blame others for why our lives are stuck in groundhogs day. Making someone else responsible for why we are not where we want to be is the nifty little mind trick we humans like to use to evade change and buy ourselves more time to stay the same.

. . .

This brings me to the "C" word.

Comfort.

Our desire for comfort can wreck our dreams faster than we can say, "I'm stuck."

Rest assured, my friends, this has been my story more days than I would know how to count. There are times —years even, where I felt like no matter what I did, I could not seem to get my life going in the direction I wanted it to go in. Looking back over the last couple of decades, I have made massive changes in my life trajectory, which have brought me to the place of joy, fulfillment, and success that I live in today, professionally and with my family. However, before every change, there was always something tempting me to stay the same—my damn comfort zone. Comfort whispers the promise that I won't have to be afraid, that I don't need to risk anything, that no one's going to laugh at me, and that I won't let anyone down. Comfort also lures me in and keeps me the same by reminding me how impossible it feels for me to change or how much easier it would be to lower my standard so that I didn't have to feel accountable for my dreams coming true.

. . .

Here is what comfort doesn't tell you —staying the same isn't real. There's no such thing. You are either growing or shrinking, but nothing stays the same. We all know that no matter how quiet we try to be or how low we set our standards-- we still feel afraid. We continue to deal with feelings of uncertainty, and we're still concerned about criticism. The irony is painful.

Probably one of my most significant realizations was seeing how my comfort zone holds me back. I've always had big dreams. Guess where the achievement of those dreams exists? Outside of my comfort zone. Every time.

I'll never forget how terrified and excited I was getting on a plane for the first time in my life.

To travel halfway across the world.

For six weeks.

By myself.

I had to wrestle my comfort zone to the ground and practically knock it out to get myself to take every action it took to go on that trip.

. . .

I have always had wild and crazy ideas for my life; My first colossal leap happened then --at 19. I wanted to master my craft as a hairstylist with some of the best. It required me to do things I had never done, including flying and living in another country for a bit. I don't know if you can relate to this, but if you're a dreamer, which I know you are, there can be moments in your life where you get an idea, and it becomes an obsession. Well, at least that's what happens to me. I had this idea to become the best hairstylist I could be. I knew the only way I could do that was to do what others were unwilling to do. I saved every single dime I had and applied at Tony and Guy in London. At the time, I worked at one of the most outstanding Bay Area salons as a hairstylist just starting out. I was also going to college and living with six roommates.

I researched and wrote out an exact plan of what it would take for me to get to London for six weeks. For me to make it happen, I'd have to live on a TIGHT budget. I had just enough money to eat Top Ramen, mixed vegetables, and peanut butter and jelly sandwiches for six months. I could pay for rent and school expenses. I saved every other penny. I worked overtime, picked up side jobs, and did whatever it took to make this trip happen. The night before leaving, I was saying my goodbyes to all my coworkers. One of the company owners, Debbie, came up to me and said,

"You're not taking those scissors, are you? And what about your blow dryer and your cases…?" She went on and on. I realized I'd been so focused on getting there; I hadn't even considered how subpar the tools were I was taking with me. Before panic could fully set in, my boss smiled and gave me her most expensive scissors, brand new blow dryer, new combs, and clips. She had gone out and bought me an entire set of the nicest tools a girl could ever want. She pretended like she just had them sitting in the back closet. I knew she had gotten them for me. I guarded those gems with my life. I remember to this day the words she left me with. "Anna, you need to know you are already going to be the best because it's in you. You are not going to learn anything you don't already know about hair, but you are going to learn a whole lot about yourself. Get em' girl, and when you come back, I'm giving you one of those Euro haircuts, the ones with the short rat chewed bangs. Oh my god, you will look so cute." She was right; I learned more about myself in those six weeks than I had in my first 19 years of life. The biggest takeaway was how critical it would be for me to keep pushing myself out of my comfort zone to make my dreams happen.

My comfort zone was nowhere in sight when that plane went wheels up. If I had stayed in my comfort zone, I would've never done what it took to get on that plane and have the incredible experiences that I got to have. That trip set it in stone for me—the power of setting goals and creating a plan. The realization I could go anywhere in life I chose, set entirely in.

Fast forward to the many times I would get stuck and push back on "executing my plan" and then "not getting where I wanted to go" confused the crap out of me. I became obsessed with getting unstuck. Did I begin digging into why the hell I would lose steam or self-sabotage dreams with inaction? No.

Was I lazy? No! I worked my ass off.

Most of us are not lazy. Staying in our comfort zone isn't about not working hard or not being willing to be disciplined or stick to a plan. Our comfort zone is like this friend with really good intentions. A friend that just wants to follow you around all the time and keep you safe. Somewhat sweet but mostly annoying. The part of us that just doesn't want us to get hurt or be let down or let others down. The comfort zone intends to stick to what it already knows, even if everything that it already knows sucks because at least it knows what to expect. Considering this book is explicitly addressing those of us that desire to be dreamers and achievers. It should be noted that the comfort zone is the mothership that will always keep a dreamer dreaming but never achieving.

Tell me if I'm wrong, but I don't know if there's anybody that's more frustrated than a dreamer who feels like they can't make it happen? Here's my thought. If you're not a dreamer and you're not even thinking about these dreams in your head and ideas that you want to see come to fruition, you're not going to feel let down. A dreamer who doesn't feel like they can ever achieve the dreams inside them is like a person who's been given a fantastic virtual tour of their dream vacations but never once gets to visit a single place in person. Torture. A dreamer can only dream for so long before the dreams become painful if they don't feel like they can achieve them. I think dreaming is a critical part of achieving. I love talking about dreams and writing them down, and getting excited with each new detail.

I remember sitting on my bed as a young child and creating dreams that seemed impossible.

Dreams so big that I even scared myself with how big they were.

My favorite access to dreaming was through magazines and collaging. I spent an entire week once and collaged, with god knows how many magazines, every square inch of my bedroom walls. I surrounded myself with reminders of what I wanted in life. I was a small-town girl determined to live out big dreams. Boy, have I done just that, but not without having to silence the voice in my head so many times that would try so hard to hold me back.

Anna, you are not good enough to go to this next level.

Anna, you are not worthy of receiving so many good things in life.

Anna, who are you to want to have it all.

Somewhere along the way, I had developed an internal sense of unworthiness that kept my comfort zone pretty rigid. I believed that I needed to earn my seat at every table. It was as if I needed to prove to everyone that I was good enough to be there. I became very comfortable running myself ragged by overachieving, not saying no, and feeling like there was no end in sight. My comfort zone ensured that I was the busiest person I knew-- feeling the furthest from their dreams coming to fruition.

It wasn't until I hit a complete burnout that I stopped and noticed the trajectory of my life. It's no easy task to have it all. Lose it all. And realize who you are truly meant to be. This book is me sharing the crucial steps I took to rebuild, recover, and redesign my life my way. When you choose to live your life on your terms, you learn what stepping out of your comfort zone means. I hope this book brings light to a life of possibilities. I'm all about dreaming, designing, and creating, but you never actually know what you are capable of until you choose to act.

There are 8 fundamental lessons that have helped me live outside of my comfort zone, giving me the life I enjoy today. These lessons took me from dreaming into achieving every time. The best part of sharing what I have learned is that you can take the information and immediately apply it for instant results no matter what place you are in. I have created a fun takeaway at the end of each chapter. These exercises are not to just read through and move on. I didn't write them to just write them. The exercises are meant to help you go deeper. I know you are reading this book because you believe in your dreams. If anything in the world works to explore your true dreams, it's good old paper and pencil. Do yourself a favor and do the darn work!

This book is for you. I see you. All of you. The you that's ready to step out and up to what you were created to be. Dreamers can be achievers. "Keep Going!"

"You want something you have never had? Well, it sure isn't found in the comfort zone you are in." - *Anna Ennis*

PEP TALK

Comfort, cake, and Netflix are fun but if you are stuck doing it to avoid what you are really meant to do, get up right now! ! Not tomorrow. Right now. 3. 2. 1. You can do one thing in this very moment to move one step closer to your dream.... do these takeaways below, babe.

COMFORT ZONE
EXERCISE

- Make a list of everything you are used to in your life right now personally. (Comfort Zone)
- Make a list of everything you are used to in your life right now professionally. (Comfort Zone)
- Make a list of dreams you want to achieve PERSONALLY.
- Circle the TOP 3 most critical personal dreams.
- Now write down the 3 things you could start doing right now that would move you in the direction of making those dreams happen.
- Make a list of the dreams you want to achieve PROFESSIONALLY.
- Circle the TOP 3 most critical professional dreams.
- Now write down the 3 things you could start doing right now that would move you in the direction of making those dreams happen.
- Take a moment to see if any of the actions you wrote down to move you closer to your dreams are inside of your comfort zone?
- Schedule the actions you are going to take in your calendar.

CHAPTER 2

THE REAL
STARTING
BLOCK

BELIEFS ARE THE GATEKEEPERS THAT WILL KEEP YOU GOING OR STOP YOU DEAD IN YOUR TRACKS.

- Anna Ennis

2. THE REAL STARTING BLOCK

BEFORE ACHIEVING, BEFORE DREAMING, WE FIND beliefs. Beliefs are the gatekeepers that will keep you going or stop you dead in your tracks. Beliefs are the thoughts we hold true in the conscious and unconscious mind. They are the framework that we use to decide what's real and what's possible or not possible in our own lives. These don't have to be rational. Often, the funkiest beliefs I have are the ones that I discover when I keep doing something that's messing up my life again and again. When I notice that I continue to get an outcome in life that's making me crazy - I can always find a belief underneath that's steering me in the wrong direction. If I desire to be successful and happy, but I believe at my core that I am unworthy of success or happiness, then we have a problem. Beliefs always win. Beliefs trump logic and rationale whenever left unexamined. Let's take the belief of unworthiness that I had for the majority of my life. Rationally there was nothing unworthy about me.

I had always been a good kid, tried hard, worked hard, dreamed hard, and showed up for others. At a young age, I had an abnormally good head on my shoulders and was conscious about making the right decisions as an adult--same. The only difference as an adult--I tried even harder, worked even harder, dreamed even harder, and showed up for others. Nonetheless, underneath it all, I was plagued with feeling like nothing I ever did, said, or showed up for was good enough. Why? Because in my core, my deepest darkest beliefs, I just wasn't good enough. And no matter how much I achieved, I found myself feeling like I needed to do more somehow and be more to prove that I deserved my achievements. God, I wanted to quit. But I kept going. This treadmill kicked my ass. The funny thing is I didn't question this belief as possibly being untrue. I didn't even ask myself where it came from. That's the thing about beliefs; they just hang out in the subtle backdrop, single-handedly orchestrating your reality but yet simultaneously going completely unnoticed. Eventually, the shit hits the fan, or something in our life happens that makes us begin to question things about ourselves on a deeper level. I've had a lot happen in life that made me pause and ask what the heck was going on, but it wasn't until something catastrophic unfolded that brought me ultimately to the end of myself that I truly began my self-discovery.

I remember the first time I had a massive panic attack while driving on my daily hour and a half commute to the fantastic salon that I had been with from the ground up. As I sat on the side of the road, gripping the steering wheel, unable to breathe, an elephant on my chest, ringing in my ears with the world closing in around me--it was then I knew that I could not go on internally the way that I had been. I'd love to say that I had an insightful realization through a calm self-analysis, but no. It didn't go down like that, and this was the first of many to follow. I could not drive myself to work for over six months because the panic attacks kept coming and were so debilitating I could no longer ignore what had been building up inside me. Externally at that point in my career, I was a top leader in my industry and responsible for high-level training inside of the company as it had grown into a multi-million dollar powerhouse. I was a go-to person for answers. Everyone knew they could count on me and that I could help. I had positioned myself in a perpetual state of overdrive. No one knew that on the inside, I felt more overwhelmed than I even had words for. My husband was driving me to and from work at 4:30 AM

with our two baby girls sleeping in the back seat. I grappled with why this was happening to me. Work was my safe place. But, as soon as I got home, I was a mess. There were days I could not get out of bed. Days where I locked myself in my house. Doing the simplest of tasks felt near impossible. My husband pulled the weight for both of us at home. Not once did he ever blame or accuse me of being crazy. See, my husband and I had something happen that had brought me to my knees three years earlier.

I was 17 weeks pregnant on our way to find out the gender of our first baby. The excitement was just too much to handle. I had just barely stopped feeling terrified for 15 of those 17 weeks. I was so nervous about being a new mom. I'm a 3 on the Enneagram personality test, which means I tend to want to plan and control absolutely everything in every part of my life. I also must understand and know every detail. If it's not in "The Plan," my first instinct is panic. This was more of a how the hell am I ever going to be a mother panic. Some women are just so graceful with pregnancy. They love every moment of it, embrace it, and treasure each new stage. That was not me, but I was starting to get excited. As we walked into the appointment, my husband Jason, a very kind, caring, more of a quiet go-with-the-flow type, was beside himself with excitement. He had turned into this giddy, overly energetic person that I was not used to. Did I mention I was moody as hell? We found out our baby was a girl. Two days later, the doctor called us and said we needed to come in for an appointment to discuss the sonogram. We were new parents, so we thought this was part of the protocol. Upon arrival, we realized quickly that something was wrong. Our doctor was the best doctor ever. Some people just cross your path in life, and you don't realize until later how incredible they were--he was one of those. We were sent to a specialist because the measurement of our daughter's head was 100th off, and he thought it would be a good idea just to double-check. The specialist, to our shock, revealed that our daughter exhibited serious brain abnormalities. She had a blockage in her brain that wouldn't allow the liquid to circulate from her brain throughout the rest of her body. She would need immediate brain surgery after birth, and the signs were not looking good regarding how she would be born. In the grueling months to follow, we saw a specialist every other week until the last three months, becoming every week.

We heard all possible scenarios and looked at more ultrasounds and sonograms than you can even imagine. Each one kept getting worse and worse. We were prepared for the worst on the day our baby was born. There was a chance we would lose her, and living with that every day nearly took us out. We decided to have her in Sacramento at Sutter Memorial Hospital. Our baby was rushed into brain surgery less than 24 hours after being born. I had so much anxiety and was so sedated that I didn't even get to hold her until days after her surgery. Tillie was a fighter. She blew through the surgery with flying colors. We stayed in that hospital for close to a month after she was born. Well, not inside the hospital. Our awesome grandparents let us use their fifth-wheel trailer in the parking lot of the hospital. I breastfed every two hours and healed from a C-section in that tiny house on wheels, living on Costco pizzas. We spent every second we were allowed with our new baby in ICU.

Those short days felt like years. I could not allow myself to feel the pain. It was like lifting a car off of someone you love from pure adrenaline. I had to stay focused and healthy for my family, for Tillie, who was fighting for her life. I should now add that three months after giving birth to Tillie; we were pregnant with our precious daughter Taci born without complication 9 months later! However, the nightmare went on for three years for Tillie, therapists in and out of our house, doctors' appointments, and an entire unknown unfolding in front of us each day. Every ultrasound showed a child with cerebral palsy. We prepared for the worst, but God had other plans. We were blessed with the most amazing therapist, Carrie Lambert. She was in our house every single week teaching us how to not only take care of our baby but to teach our baby. As the years went on, it felt like a roller coaster. We were exhausted to the bone with two babies and stress that I still can't fully describe. We'd have success one week and a complete scare the next. It wasn't until Tillie was three years old that our doctors and entire medical support team confirmed Tillie's brain had healed itself. She not only did not have Cerebral Palsy, but she didn't have all of the other problems they assumed she would have. Other children who've had VP shunts in their brains have had tremendous challenges throughout their entire life. Tillie was healed.

This was the time in life when I began to learn who God was. I learned about the power of my mind and my babies. I learned that my relationship can go through hell and back and still make it. Tillie is a thriving 10-year-old today. She's sassy, smart, and powerful beyond words. Taci 9 holds a depth and calmness that brings peace wherever she goes. I don't know what we would do without them. We all survived.

But I didn't start to heal until the panic attacks forced me to check in on myself. I started a prayer, meditation, journaling journey, dealing with my beliefs and emotions --maybe for the first time. I had been so focused on keeping everything tightly and correctly together that I had no idea what the heck was going on inside. I had been to doctors who wanted to medicate me, and I refused. At one point, so desperate to fix me, I took a small dosage of antidepressants, but they made me feel worse. I say this with love in my heart that there are times and situations where medication is necessary. I just knew for my case, this was inner healing that needed to surface. At the time, I had no idea how this would happen. I had this constant voice telling me that this was happening for me, not to me. It's the one thing that kept me from going under. I've done and been through hard things in my life, and I recognize that voice. But deep down, I was so disconnected from my own body that I had no idea how or why this was happening. Of course, I went to google as we all do to self diagnose. I was introduced to this whole new world of what anxiety and panic attacks really were. This thing called meditation kept coming up. It was the only non-medication thing I could find. So...I decided to look deeper into it. I'm an achiever, so of course, I did this obsessive thing of immersion. I set up a small area in my closet to meditate three or more times a day. And by meditate, I meant sitting in my closet with the lights off cross-legged, trying to calm my mind with ocean music playing in the background. It was a start. Sometimes I would use it as a place to just cry in silence and release emotion. Other days I just sat. Day after day, I noticed that I could calm my brain for a minute or two at a time. For this over-thinker, I would take it. I would go into my dark closet and would come out feeling an ounce of hope. When you feel a glimpse of "I might be able to make it out of this," you know it's bigger than yourself. I then found every book, video, audio I could find on how this all worked. I began to study the brain, energy, and faith. It was fascinating. I began to learn just why our body shuts down and ways we can heal ourselves. To this very day, I choose to continue to further my education on our bodies because it's magical how awesome we are as humans.

Learning how to silence my mind is something that I work on to this day. Some days I'm stellar and can go forever. On other days I have to go back to square one. Silencing your mind allows you to connect to that voice deep down. Connecting with God, your higher source, the universe, or whatever faith you choose to practice is one of the most humbling parts of being human.

Life has a way of holding you accountable to your heart's desire and giving you endless opportunities to heal, change, and grow. I am not sure that if everything hadn't completely exploded inside of me-- I would have ever stopped, sat down, and got to work on my beliefs. I began to question my feelings of unworthiness sincerely. I began to ask myself why it was that I felt incapable of celebrating any of my victories? I was determined to gain new beliefs about myself and life that accurately reflected the life I wanted to live.

I wanted to help people on a deeper level on a greater scale. I wanted to be a part of something bigger than myself that made a difference in the world for the better. I wanted time freedom and financial freedom to spend far more time with my family than I was currently able.

As I became more precise about what I wanted to achieve in life, I began to see what beliefs I had inside that had gone unquestioned and were sabotaging my goals.

It was almost as if just by actively acknowledging beliefs that didn't align with my true life goals, I began to dismantle them. Negative beliefs I had about myself could no longer pop up without me noticing. This awareness allowed me to start mindfully, changing how I believed, which began to change my reality. Over time I realized I had nothing to prove as long as I genuinely accepted myself; the rest would fall into place. Changing my limiting beliefs kept me going and keeps me going to this day.

I say to those of you ready to put in the work, changing your beliefs is the best starting point. Sometimes we have so many stories we have told ourselves that it can be difficult to determine our beliefs that limit our lives.

Your beliefs become your thoughts,
Your thoughts become your words,
Your words become your actions,
Your actions become your habits,
Your habits become your values,
Your values become your destiny.

— *Mahatma Gandhi* —

AZ QUOTES

PEP TALK

What's holding you back is sometimes hidden deep down in the darkest places of our heart. When we chose to realize that something could be different in ourselves, we take the first step. It's worth it to put in the work for yourself. Ten minutes of your time can be the ten minutes that changes it all.

EXERCISE ON BELIEFS

- Make a list of anything you think is holding you back from achieving the dreams you listed in the Comfort Zone Exercise in Chapter 1.
- Read through the list as if they are all limiting beliefs and write a new belief next to each one.
  - Example:
    - Old belief: I don't have enough money to make my dreams come true.
    - New belief: There is more than enough money coming my way to make my dreams come true I'm excited to see all the places it comes from!

CHAPTER 3

NOT GONNA CRASH & BURN

THE FEAR OF
FAILURE
DOESEN'T HAVE
TO HOLD YOU
BACK.
YOU CAN BE
AFRAID TO FAIL
AND STILL
KEEP GOING.

- Anna Ennis

3. NOT GONNA CRASH & BURN

NEW DREAMS + NEW GOALS = NEW FEARS BIGGEST fear: what if I fail?

I'm sorry, not sorry, I loath failing. There is nothing that has made me want NOT to KEEP GOING more than feeling like I failed. No matter how many times I've heard some of the most successful people in the world saying, "failure is part of success, " it's never made it feel good. To this day, it pisses me off when I fail at something. BUT something powerful has happened--my fear of failure no longer holds me back. So you can be afraid to fail and still keep going. In the old days, I would feel scared to fail; it would cause me to procrastinate. I just couldn't bring myself to take action on various goals because this looming idea that I might fail felt catastrophic. Often times what would happen is I would leave things to the very last minute, and then I would get the thing done just in the nick of time. The amount of stress that I felt would sometimes keep me up at night, worrying about what would happen if I failed. Here is the magic bullet I discovered (drum roll, please); just keep doing it, afraid. Sometimes I'd fail, but most of the time, I didn't, and over time I had enough success under my belt to realize that it would always be worth it to me to risk failing no matter how afraid I was. The only thing that scared me more was not actualizing my dreams, and if that meant that I had to fall even a bunch of times before I got there --then so be it. Something else happened. I began to procrastinate less and less. However, the fear of failure stayed with me; my confidence to persevere continued to increase. Sometimes you can get bucked off the horse, making it really scary to get back on. You might have an experience in your past that made you doubt yourself because things didn't turn out the way you thought it would, and it felt like a failure.

I remember one specific experience that shaped my adolescent years more than any other. I had the best fourth-grade teacher ever. Mrs. Loomis was not only the coolest, but she was also our Student Council and Leadership teacher. She had such a positive impact on me that I promised myself that I would be on Student Council when I entered sixth grade. Nearing sixth grade, I was approached by Mrs. Loomis and asked if I wanted to attend a leadership conference with kids from all over the United States near where we lived. I had never done anything like that before, but I could feel my heart beat faster, knowing that I wanted to do it. She said if I went, I would have all of the needed skills to run for office. Come to find out, no other kids from our school were going, so in my mind, that meant I had a sure ticket to victory. Class Secretary, here I come! The Leadership camp was that summer, and it cost $500. She had graciously offered to pay for $200 of it if I could raise the rest of the money. I had babysat a good portion of my childhood, but now I had to get down to business. I had a huge goal. I was 12 now, and I decided I was ready for a job. I worked almost every weekend to raise that money as a hostess at a café. This will age me, but at that time, wages were around three dollars an hour. Do the math--I worked a lot of hours. It felt so good to make enough money to go. I was off to camp for five days that summer! I was petrified. Not only was I the only person from my entire school, but all of the other kids were from all other parts of the country. They were all older and so loud. At the time, I was a more reserved 12-year-old, but I showed up.

I participated. I even had fun. I returned to school as a seventh-grader ready for elections. I campaigned. I rallied. I was determined to be the next class Secretary. It was just assumed. I had set a goal and put in the work.

But… little did I know that I would have competition. A friend in my circle of friends ran also. I had told myself that I had already won. Not the type of "I've already won because you're positive thinking, and you've done all the work." No, it was the "I've already won because my ego has taken over" type, which we all know where that lands us. On the day of the elections, I was a mess. I was the most nervous I had ever been. I just knew that because I had attended the Leadership camp that everything was in the bag. I had a one-up on the other candidate. Wrong. The other candidate had younger, loud siblings, who she paid off with candy. (Middle school marketing tactic I didn't see coming). They told all of their friends to vote for their sister, and to my surprise on the announcement on the loudspeaker the next day-- she won. She had won because she got more people to vote for her.

I was crushed. I had tried so hard, and it definitely felt like failure. I felt cloaked in it, but I learned something. Ugh. Yes, I learned something that has been one of my single most significant ingredients for my success today.

Although I was focused on criteria for the position and feeding my ego, I had forgotten entirely about actually telling enough people and self-promoting. Words of wisdom… No matter how smart you are, how much you think you fit the position, the things you have achieved… it all boils down to people. And knowing a whole grip load of them. Connections with people matter more than the title on your name. I know this as a fact today because my professional and personal relationships have been vital in every good thing that's happened to date. So yes. We fail--all of us. Spoiler alert...not trying is a form of failing. The ironic news? The only way to guarantee failure is by not trying. If you try, you have a chance to learn and succeed. If you don't try, you have zero chance of succeeding. When I'm terrified, I'm going to crash and burn, I just bite the bullet and hit the gas. If I fail, it won't be because I didn't go down without a fight. It won't be because I sat on the sidelines with the peanut gallery. If I fail, I'll be pissed, and I'll be proud, and I'll probably learn something that will add to my treasure chest life-wisdom-nuggets. No matter how hard you think you've failed, you can ALWAYS get back up and keep going. If you let yourself see it, I guarantee you're even smarter and stronger because of it. Today, I realize things don't always work out how I envisioned them, but I can tell you for sure they always work out.

> "I can accept failure and be pissed, but the guilt of not actually trying is infuriating." -*Anna Ennis*

PEP TALK

Yes, trying and sucking is a freaking bummer. Trying and falling on your face feels even worse. But, wouldn't you rather try than be eaten up inside with unrealized possibility? Being mad as hell goes away. The resentment of giving up before you even start goes with you to your grave.

These questions below may bring some emotion out, but dude, trust me...go for it!

EXERCISE ON FAILING

- Write down your top 3 most significant, most gut-wrenching failures that you believe are holding you back:
- Now write down the diamond lesson you learned from each failure and the positive impact it's had on your life: *Pro-tip: Don't write something ridiculous like "I learned I couldn't trust people." That's lazy, find something really good so you can KEEP GOING!

CHAPTER 4

WHEN BELIEVING BECOMES ACHIEVING

DREAMS
BECOME A
REALITY
"OFFICIALLY"
WHEN WE TAKE
ACTION.
ACTION IS THE
YELLOW BRICK
ROAD FROM
BELIEVING TO
ACHIEVING.

- Anna Ennis

4. WHEN BELIEVING BECOMES ACHIEVING

As I began to intentionally live outside of my comfort zone, overhaul my beliefs, and get beyond my fear of failure, my life started to change for the better rapidly. I think it's important to note here that it still felt rough from time to time—but not because things were going wrong but because things were going right. (Sheesh, can't we just be happy lol!) Each new opportunity that showed up came with new challenges and unknowns. I want to take a second to focus on the fact that when opportunities presented themselves to me, they felt scary more times than not. I think a lot of people can get confused by this. I know that it used to confuse me. Praying, praying, praying that something was going to show up so that I could move the needle in my own life. Then something would show up! A door would swing wide open, and instead of running through it filled with gratitude and excitement--I would find myself wanting to hit the brakes and find a reason to not walkthrough. It makes perfect sense to quit when we feel like we are losing but quitting when we are winning is more common than you might think. It's essential to notice specific triggers that can keep us stuck. Today, I am prepared for the part of me that feels nervous about new opportunities showing up, and because I am aware of the little voice in my head that says don't walk through the door, stay where you are, and stay safe, I have trained myself just to keep going:)

Dreams become a reality "officially" when we take action. Action is the yellow brick road from believing to achieving. Walking through the door or crawling through the doggy door of opportunity--whatever you need to DO--you gotta do it. There are no shortcuts to taking action. Yes, we can work smarter, not harder, but it's a "doing-thing," not a "thinking-thing." It's all steps. The great news--everything is one step at a time. Even if you are a total badass, and I know you are because those are my people, it's still one step at a time. The best of the best DO NOT MULTITASK OR SKIP STEPS. In fact, they just embraced this reality early on, took the damn steps, and that's why they are where they are today. They just kept going, taking one step, or writing one page, or returning one email at a time. As a dreamer, I have an unlimited amount of ideas that pop into my head each day. It's nuts. I feel like an idea machine sometimes; most dreamers are idea machines, but the dream becomes a reality only after taking action. I could never "DO" all of the ideas that light me up, and I have learned--that is 100% ok. They are meant to inspire me, not to distract or confuse me. I had a come-to-Jesus with myself when I realized I would use dreaming sometimes to avoid action because I was afraid to take the next step. I dream all the time still, but I am always clear on what dreams I'm building versus which ones I'm just playing in my head.

This brings me to "messy action." It's 100% great to take messy action! Sometimes I'm not sure which dreams to start building, so I just start taking action--messy action. It doesn't need to be perfect because if it did, I would never take action. I have had to fight off perfectionism since I can remember, and dear lord--she is just a nightmare; literally, NOTHING IS EVER GOOD ENOUGH FOR HER. But seriously, trying to take the perfect action to avoid mistakes will only make it impossible to keep going. Action is to dreams what oxygen is to fire-completely necessary.

The real breakthrough came when I realized I could do "hard things." I read this excellent book called Untamed by Glennon Doyle. I keep going back to this phrase she writes, "We can do hard things."

I have had to remind myself of this many times the past six months. When I'm feeling the stress of my marriage, kids, business, life, global pandemics, or things feeling upside down, I bring myself right back to momentum with those five words "We can do hard things." I can do hard things.

Mamas out there, you know the toll having children takes on your body. Let's talk about hard things for a minute. I went after a dream of living in a body that was stronger, healthier and more fit. It was by far the most challenging place to start but the most important place to start for all other things to happen in my life. I had wanted to make the changes for a long time. Here's the hard part for some dreams. You don't realize your true potential until you step out into a place that can feel a bit lonely—a place where stuff starts to come up for you. Working an excessive amount of hours, being a mom, wife, and maintaining a crazy busy schedule, there felt like no time for my health and well-being to happen consistently. Overall I would've measured myself as a healthy person.

Here's what I had to ask myself: Was I active? Did I start the day with myself first or push myself consistently every single day? When I sat down and looked at what I was doing for myself versus what I was telling myself I was doing-- it was a completely different story. My husband had completed 75 hard with

Andy Frisella. You do five specific things every single day for 75 days. When you read over the five things, you think, oh my gosh, this is a cinch. When you actually get into it, and life happens, you realize it's a lot harder to be there for yourself than you had ever imagined. This came up for me.

My husband had gotten massive results, and I saw him transform in front of my eyes. After resistance and watching him for an entire year, I wanted to feel as great as he did. I don't know how many times he encouraged me to start or to put myself first, but as you know, unless it's our idea, we ain't doing it.

I did three 75 hards in one year. I share this because it was and still is the hardest thing I've taken on for myself. No pun intended. It's 75 days straight of showing up for you first before anyone else in your life. Did I feel like I let a ton of people down by putting myself first? Heck yes, I did. Did I cry most days in the beginning? Absolutely. Were there some days that I showed up in the pouring rain? Yes!

My life has changed dramatically by choosing to choose discipline for my daily habits. The door has been cracked, and I can see a little sliver of my potential when I don't break promises to myself. What keeps me going is the way I feel inside about myself. Yes, I look in the mirror, and I'm definitely more fit than I was a year ago, but that's not what drives me harder. What drives me harder is that I feel a little more like myself. I'm seeing the impact it has on others around me by choosing to do what others are not willing to do. I see the lives I'm changing by just staying in my lane. Others are seeing and giving themselves permission to do the same. I laughed at my Grandma when she said it takes one person to change the world by just doing what they were created to do. I never really understood that I am changing the world by following what was put in my heart. It couldn't be more evident today.

> "At the center of your being you have the answer; you know who you are and you know what you want." – *Lao Tzu*

Hard things have driven me through places I didn't know I was capable of pushing myself through.

Doing hards things can put us in that space of reevaluation, resulting in what we like to call "personal growth."

Hard things help us revisit our purpose, lives, dreams, and make sure it's all on track. Dreaming becomes achieving with action. The more we embody this notion and do hard things-- the faster we hit our goals. I don't think life has to be hard for it to count. I'm not a martyr. I'm not in denial either. Some actions I take are a breeze, and some steps I take, make me want to cuss and quit. When I signed up for my best life, I said yes to it all because as much as I love to dream, I love to see my dreams come to life even more.

"You don't have to be perfect or even ready to start, but you do have to start before you even know what it feels like to be ready." -*Anna Ennis*

PEP TALK

Let's talk! Hard things will try to stop you whenever you take the first steps of action toward your dream. Be ready. They are coming if they haven't already arrived. Facing hard things is where your core and character will be tested. It's on the other side of you not giving up that you see what's really possible. Just over the hump of hard is momentum. When you feel just an ounce of it, you will be on fire. Moral of the story "You don't have to know what the hell you are doing to start," but you do have to take messy, imperfect action to even get in the arena. What's it gonna hurt? The first step is to take a few minutes and answer the questions below for yourself. You're welcome. I love you.

EXERCISE

- What are 3 actions you know you need to take to make your life better?
- For each action, write down how that action will help you.
- Give yourself a deadline to complete each action.
- Tag me on social media #IdiditAnna, and I'll know we are in this together, and we can follow each other's journey.

CHAPTER 5

CAN BE VS. MUST BE

MOST OF US
NEED TO BE A
LITTLE MORE
UNREASONABLE.
WITHOUT EVEN
REALIZING IT,
WE CAN SHOVE
OURSELVES
INTO A
REASONABLE
SMALL BOX.

- Anna Ennis

5. CAN BE VS. MUST BE

I BELIEVE WITH ALL MY HEART THAT WE CAN BE anything we want to be. I hate when people tack on "within reason" following that statement. Nope. Most of us need to be a little more unreasonable. Without even realizing it, we can shove ourselves into our reasonable small box that has been pre-designed by family, friends, culture, etc. and "reason" ourselves into a crappy job or a life that feels grey. I want my two daughters to dream big, make as many mistakes as needed to get to where their hearts lead. We are raising them this way, and yes, they make me crazy when they draw on the walls of their rooms to bring to life a new idea.

I have so many Tillie and Taci stories being my most outstanding teachers on "dreaming big and doing life full throttle." Most of them involve great big messes. I have been tempted to stuff them in reasonable little boxes when they haven't stopped talking to me for hours on end, their creative projects have turned the house upside down, and my tank is on empty, and they have at least three quarters left. Sure, I want to have peace and quiet and maybe even some white furniture, but you know what? I refuse to force them to shrink down so that I can feel more comfortable. It's tough to watch your child have a dream or an idea and go for it and see their face when it doesn't pan out. It's tempting to guide them to only go all-in on things they are guaranteed to "succeed" at from our vantage point.

The real issue here is that we are already hard-wired for "playing it safe," and we know it takes a lot to be outside of our comfort zones, so I have tried my darndest to be the voice in my little girls' life that cheers "Dust it off and keep going! Create-on! Dream on!". This is the very same voice that I have had to cultivate in myself to keep me going. I learned something fundamental along the way. It's important to believe you can be anything you want to, but it's even more important to clarify what you MUST BE. The "can be" part opens you up to a world of possibilities to explore, which is fun and interesting. The "must be" part is when you decide who you want to become. When you know who you want to become and put a stake in the ground-- it becomes a MUST. This creates massive amounts of energy behind the idea. You will begin to take action you may not have taken before because you know who you must become. I look back and remember thinking I must become the person who manages her life with confidence, leads myself, my family, and others to more in life. I must become the person who has the freedom to give of my time and resources—making a positive impact! I must. Not I can be, hopefully, will be, will try to be. I decided I must be. I began to make decisions that I thought that version of myself would make. I found mentors to emulate no matter how out of place I felt.

I surrounded myself with people who showed up the way I wanted to even if I was panicked about it. In the beginning stages of my path to a healthier body, I did lots of walking outside because it felt like I could connect to the world. If I'm sincere, it was the least intimidating way of exercising. One day when I was on a walk, I remember getting hit with one huge insight nugget. Anna, what if you lost everything in your life? Would you still be happy? Was happiness a maybe? I decided happiness was an inside job and not contingent on fair weather circumstances.

There comes moments when we have these substantial disconnected thoughts about who we are and who we want to be. We put up these boundaries and barriers that until we make this much money, weigh this weight, or are this type of a mom or wife; we aren't going to live up to the person we imagined in our minds.

This thought hit me like a lightning bolt. "Yes, I could be happy" sounded like an option that was based on a maybe if all the dots lined up. If I had the amount of money I needed first, well-behaved kids, a husband who didn't drive me crazy, then I "could be" happy.

But what if I said to myself, "I must choose" happiness even though the physical states of my life had not quite aligned yet. What if my happiness was based less on objective? What if happiness shows up in the pursuit and less in the actual receiving part? I must be happy before I can receive and appreciate anything good that comes my way.

When you decide who you MUST become, I'm telling you it changes everything if you just keep going.

YOU NEED TO
UNDERSTAND
THAT LIFE
ISN'T WHAT
YOU'RE GIVEN,
IT'S WHAT YOU
CREATE,
WHAT YOU
CONQUER
AND WHAT YOU
AIM TO ACHIEVE

- Agekills

PEP TALK

You can. You will. You must. Guys...let's be real here until you draw the line in the sand of what must happen; you ain't going anywhere. Take it from someone who realized this the hard way. Our standard for ourselves is far more important than the standards others put on us. This is where it gets intense-the part where you get to define your life. Must, means you may mess up, but you will always find your way back to the stake you planted in the ground.

EXERCISE

- Who MUST you become? Write about her (you) in detail.
- How does she act?
- Is there any pattern you have in your life that doesn't fit who you must become? If so, write about what you must do instead and take action.

CHAPTER 6

ON THE EDGE

NOW IS THE
WAKE-UP TIME! IF
YOU ARE ON THE
EDGE, IT IS TIME
FOR YOU TO
JUMP.

- Anna Ennis

6. ON THE EDGE

SO YOU'RE RIGHT THERE STRAIGHT...ALMOST...SO CLOSE to taking some serious action. You've had some fantastic dreams you have thought of doing. Maybe for a long time. Perhaps you've dabbled. Maybe you tried once and felt nervous going all in. No matter what has happened in your past, you're starting to feel like it's now or never. The only problem is you're looking for a third option because "now" sounds terrible and "never" sounds even worse. What about "someday"? Someday feels better right? Like, right now would be crazy because you would have to take action and be uncomfortable, and it's scary. Never is devastating, so that doesn't feel good at all. Someday is perfect! We think to ourselves, "I don't have to take any action, and I can keep dreaming!". You know what I'm saying right now. Shut the front door. Someday is a load of crap. I'm not trying to be dramatic when I say someday might as well be never. You have to confront this. Someday will lull you to sleep, so you don't feel your dreams die. That is the truth. Now is the wake-up time! If you are on the edge, it is time for you to jump.

TAKE THE ACTIONS YOU NEED TO TAKE! And don't say, "I don't know what to do." That someday's best friend. Someday and I-don't-know-what-to-do, sit around together just talking while life passes them by. They are lame, and you need to get the hell away from them because they want to keep you feeling stuck. YOU ARE NOT STUCK. YOU ARE SCARED—two very different things. Stuck is being pinned underneath a boulder in the middle of a desert. Anything short of that--you are surrounded by opportunity! For crying out loud, we are in the information age. We have the internet.

I have learned more from Youtube alone than I ever thought possible. There are a bazillion online groups of amazing people that want nothing more than to connect and collaborate. You just have to go for it! When I decided to go full entrepreneur and transition my career of 17 years in corporate America while also being the primary breadwinner for my family-you bet your ass, I was terrified. I know all about "someday" because I told myself someday I'll own my own business for about ten years longer than I had planned. Here's the crazy part. I was waiting until it felt safe to transition. By safe, I mean my family would not be at financial risk in any way, and I had the confidence and know-how to guarantee success. Ok, that's not the crazy part-that part makes perfect sense. The crazy part was that it never happened. There was never a point where transitioning and taking action on my dream wasn't a little (or even a lot) risky.

Further, I never felt like I knew enough or felt like I could guarantee success. When I FINALLY cut the cord, I wasn't ready, but it was time. I knew deep down that time passing was only making me feel further from my dream of owning my own company and changing lives at scale. I was waking up feeling panicked that I was going to look back and realize I missed it. This isn't an age thing either. I want to be clear--we can change lanes at any age. For me, I just knew the clock was running out on the inside. So I made the decision. I jumped by putting in my notice and went out on my own. Something unique happened; my confidence immediately started to get stronger, not because I knew what to do, but because I knew I could figure it out. All the time that I had spent thinking about it but not going all-in had chipped away my ability to trust myself. Sprinkle in a few investments gone sideways, and businesses almost started but stopped at the 11th hour just made me feel like shit. Lo and behold, when I just left the edge in a free fall -as cliche as it may sound-I really did find my wings. Initially, it was shaky, and not every decision made it more comfortable, but by God, I was flying. I wasn't letting myself down on a core level, which gave me the momentum, I had longed for.

I've had many successes as an entrepreneur. I've had big wins. Writing this part of the book has been the most rewarding part because I'm not a person who naturally sees my wins. It's taken practice for me to set the discipline of reflection. When I look back on my years as an entrepreneur, all the success moments I have involve people. It's funny the fancy, shiny and expensive goals we set for ourselves and our businesses fade away in our minds. But the stories of the lives that we have changed and the people that have changed us are the ones that stick with us. I went into business to use the skills that were given to me to help make others' lives better.

Success comes in all different forms. I can get caught up in the objective forms of success aka the cars, houses, investments, travel. It is not the deciding factor in my mind. My greatest business success is the single, newly divorced Mom who feels her value for the first time after a course she has taken from the material I created. When I see a working Mom push boundaries, she didn't know possible to get her body in shape. That's success. When a friend who has never meditated tries it for the first time and thinks she might try it again. That's success. Seeing a young girl stand up for what she believes and choose to sit at the table, she doesn't feel like she belongs. That's success. When my daughter goes against society's grain and toots her horn to a different song, that's success. I have had the opportunity to help countless men and women make their lives better by inspiring new ideas, creating action plans for their dreams, and focusing on the "musts" of their lives.

At the end of this whole ride, there will come a moment for all of us, where we get to look back and reflect on the impact we had on another's life. Real success always involves others.

"Success is the master of creating nothing into something and then teaching others how to do the same" -*Anna Ennis*

PEP TALK

Here goes--it may sting a bit, but it must be said. It's not all about you. You may think it should be but, it is possible to work on your dream and help others at the same time reach their goals. The next time that friend calls and wants to chat or the coworker invites you to coffee to share a wild idea... go. Take the time for them. Every time I am annoyed that I have to stop what I am doing to tend to something else, I get exactly what I needed. God has a funny way of lining out what we need for our success along the way. Sometimes it's in the most unexpected place. Don't get to the end and realize you wish you would have spent more time actually living and not obsessing about achieving. Take it from someone who has made that mistake. You have 10 minutes, so make it happen. Contemplate the thoughts below.

EXERCISE

- I want you to close your eyes and imagine yourself at 85 years old, and you're asked by a young family member to tell them about your life. Imagine you never left the edge and never accomplished your dreams. Tell that young family member about that version of your life. Just feel it. Confront it so that whether you decide to stay where you are or leave the edge, you know what's on the table.

- Now do the same thing again but tell the version of your life where you left the edge and accomplished your dreams. Then feel that and take action.

CHAPTER 7

YOUR BEST LIFE

YOU HAVE TO
GIVE YOURSELF
PERMISSION TO
BE YOURSELF
AND GO AFTER
WHAT TRULY
ALIGNS WITH
YOU.

- Anna Ennis

7. **YOUR BEST LIFE**

YOUR. BEST. LIFE. NOT SOMEONE ELSE'S BEST LIFE. Build your dream. I love helping people make their dreams happen. It's what makes me light up inside and feel like it's all worth it. It's this indescribable high that you get after you have helped someone achieve something they've always wanted to achieve. It's addictive. Serving others. As with any addiction, it can become a distraction. I'm going to share this sneaky thing that was happening to me for years before I realized it and got in front of it. I was so passionate about helping others build their dreams that I would get lost in it and backburner my own.

As someone who believes that giving is the key to happiness --I had to look very carefully at what was happening to see it. Every time I'd start to take a little action toward starting my business, I would suddenly say yes and give all of my time and energy to someone else's dream. I love helping, I didn't want to let people down, it made me happy to see their success, but something was off still. One day I finally realized I have never gone all-in on "my thing." I would get worried that I was being selfish and decided to help others and not myself--but I would always shelve my brand. That was the final leap for me. That was the edge I had to jump from. I knew that if I owned my brand, I'd be able to help people so much more effectively. This was my dream. This time I needed to show up and back myself. For some reason, I could show up and back my friends, family, or clients. I would jump into helping someone else instead of backing myself. I finally had to call it. Anna-that's it! You are going to build your own brand, and that's the end of it.

I was hiding behind helping others. It was the perfect alibi. I didn't feel bad about not taking action on my dreams because I was selfless. Sweet Jesus. More like another come to Jesus...No more hiding. Build your brand Anna, and then you can help others as you've always dreamed. So I cleaned up my schedule, said no to almost everything, fought off feelings of guilt, and kept going. It was time to build my dream. I found that me building my brand of taking messy action, dreaming big, and loving the shit out of yourself-has reached far more people than I was able to before!

Please hear me on this--I LOVE HELPING PEOPLE. It was never about me needing to help people less; it was about me helping me first, so I had more to give. I had never understood how important it was to help me first and go after my dream. You can imagine, with my early years of feeling so unworthy, the idea sounded sac religious.

So giving anywhere I can has only grown. Today, I make sure I'm also building my dreams too.

What happens if someone has a different dream in mind for you? It's not uncommon for parents to have a dream for their child that the child has zero interest in. It's also not unusual for that same child to grow up and build the dream his/her parents thought best instead of their own. It can happen to the best of us. Hello, it happens to most of us--until we see it and get on track with our dreams. We are going to show up the strongest for what is truly authentic to ourselves. Going after your dreams is your most generous contribution to humanity. Check out Erica Ormsby's Tedx Talk on following your dreams being imperative. Since I put my foot down and went, all-in on me, I have had more to give to my kids, husband, friends, clients, and projects that excite me. Living my "best-life" aligns with my best-self. You have to give yourself permission to be yourself and go after what truly aligns with you.

I'm always putting myself in situations where being me can feel hard. Anytime we put ourselves out there or try new things, we question whether we actually "can" do that thing, talk to that person, or show up when we don't know the outcome.

Every time I permit myself to go after it in life, I show my daughters by example what following your dreams looks like. I say if you want to make a difference, make the first change at home. Your kids are a great first starting point. Don't have kids? Well, then make it a co-worker, a friend, or a family member. It spreads like wildfire. One person living their best life gives permission to another to do the same.

"You want to make the biggest impact, go live your best life. It's contagious." *-Anna Ennis*

PEP TALK

Reality check. Whose dream are you actually building? Is it yours? Or is it what someone else wants you to do? Life takes twists and turns. Sometimes we lose track of our position and need to take a minute to reflect, redesign, and restart. Where do you measure up right now? Ask yourself the following questions below.

EXERCISE

- What does your best life look like?
- Is the dream you've been building yours? If yes, great! But if not, what can you do to start living your best life now?

Your dreams matter most. I applaud you for choosing to make the most of this life.

Thank you, and to help you make the most of taking action on your dreams for all my readers of "Keep Going!" I have a special gift for you.

Visit www.annaennis.co to claim your gift now.

CHAPTER 8
ABUNDANCE
-MIC DROP

GIVING WITH THE
BELIEF THAT
THERE IS
ALWAYS ENOUGH
IS
ABUNDANCE.

- Anna Ennis

8. ABUNDANCE--MIC DROP

I HAD NO IDEA WE WERE POOR. I NEVER FELT POOR.

Being raised by a single Mom, we had no money but felt rich in every other way. We always had enough, and I never felt like I was going without. There are many badass single parents out there, and if a single parent has raised you, you truly realize the magnitude of how extraordinary it is. I'm married to a husband who ultimately takes the reins more often than not when it comes to raising our children. And I sometimes take it for granted when I think about all that it takes to raise a child by yourself.

When I look back at my childhood, I have nothing but fond memories. We never had fancy food, the latest toys, or fashion. Again, clueless because I had a blast. I know one specific thing that our family did that always reminded me that we had plenty. We served others. I had a great perspective because we paid attention to others' needs and gave anywhere we could. To me, I felt rich. It wasn't until someone mentioned all we didn't have that I even noticed.

My mom worked 2 to 3 jobs most of my childhood, following my parent's separation and eventual divorce. My Mom was and still is a rockstar; she handled it all-- house, bills, and never missed a single sports event. As I write this, I'm flooded with gratitude all over again. However, the most powerful lesson she taught my brother and I was the power of giving. We didn't wait for someone to ask us for help. We jumped in where we could. We always knew we had something to offer.

She would be dead dog tired, and it was undeniable, but she still found time and resources to give to someone even less fortunate than us. At times, I remember not having a ton of food in our cupboards, and my Mom was cooking for the neighbor kids whose parents never cooked for them. She was the master of turning nothing into something. She was a real example of abundance. Always enough to go around.

The connection between giving and abundance has become profoundly evident throughout my life. This thing happens when we serve. We forget about our problems or circumstances or even our failures. Human connection happens, and we focus on what matters. My

Mom has literally given the shirt off of her back for someone before. Her example made me rich before I ever made a single dollar.

Giving with the belief that there is always enough is abundance. Here is my experience with having an abundance mindset. I still have plenty to this day, no matter how much I give. I had something happen recently that is a great example of abundance. I was rushing into a Party City store to grab some party favors for this fun little thing for my daughters. I overheard a young boy, maybe 10years old, crying as he ran into the store, panicking saying, "someone stole my bike!" He was so upset. I cut out of line from the cash register and caught his attention, asking if he wanted to use my phone to call his parents? His eyes were red from fighting off tears. He called his Grandma to come and pick him up, telling her what had happened. Long story short, I learned that the boy had worked really hard to earn money to buy a Halloween costume that he wanted so badly. He had saved just enough that day and had ridden his bike to buy the costume. When he came back out of the store, his bike was gone. I felt heartbroken for the boy as I drove home. It took me back to that feeling that I had at his age when my bike was stolen. I could not get the devastated look in his eyes out of my head. The boy had used my phone to call his Grandma, so I had her phone number. I called her and let her know that

I would like to buy her Grandson a new bike. She couldn't believe it and said she was just thinking she didn't know how she could ever get him a new bike. It sounded like she was raising him on her own. She was shocked and thrilled. I went to Walmart and bought him a gift card so he could pick out any bike he wanted. I felt so emotional about it all I asked my husband if he would deliver the card from us. I was told the boy was beside himself with excitement. It made my whole day to think of him happy.

I checked the mail that next week and much to my surprise, I had a check from "overpayment" from our local electric company! I wasn't surprised to see the money because this kind of unexpected thing happens to me more than I can count. I was surprised to see money come back from our electric company. Honestly, receiving money back from them would be as weird as getting a check from the DMV. I'm not saying you give with the expectation of being repaid; it's more like you give knowing there is plenty for us all, and it comes back around. I didn't think twice about spending the money for the boy's bike, and that's not because I have so much money. It doesn't matter--it's because I know that there is always plenty. That check was such a blessing and so much fun. This happens to me regularly, money comes in perfectly when I need it, or I meet the perfect person to direct me effortlessly to the next step.

When we aren't focused on what we don't have and just walk around, feeling grateful for everything we do, "our cup runneth over." Most of the time, I just know it's all working out, and everything I need and desire is finding its way to me. I do my part by taking action on what's in front of me and staying grateful. Faith has played a gigantic role in continuing to develop my abundance mindset. I know that God loves us all and has our back. Abundance is so much more than money. I will tell you that my weirdness with money was the only thing standing between me and money practically falling out of the sky. I would judge myself by how much money I had as an adult. I was worried about not having it, so I became obsessed with making it. I treated money like a bad habit. I wanted it but then felt guilty about it, so I'd hurry and get rid of it. Sometimes I hide it, but no matter what, stress about it. My Mom taught me abundance by example, but as I said, we didn't have money, so I didn't think about it. Society taught me about money, and I heard some dirty rumors that it took me years to demystify.

Here's what I heard about money…

There is not enough money.

Money is hard to make.

Money's hard to keep.

There's not enough for everyone.

Having money means you think you're better than other people.

Not having money means I'm not good enough.

Money can make people deceive you.

If you have money and others don't, you should feel ashamed.

Who am I to have money?

And maybe my favorite BS rumor:

If you are paid for helping someone, it's not giving; it's taking, so you need to do everything for free.

Shit! I'm lucky I didn't become homeless with that U-haul of confusion.

It turns out money does whatever I believe it's going to do.

If I think I don't have it, it stays away.

If I expect it to show up whenever I need it, I'm not stressin'; it just shows up.

It turns out money is everywhere and continuously flowing to me from unexpected and expected places all the time. It also turns out that every time I'm paid to do what I love, I give someone else permission to have the same abundance. It's crazy. Money hasn't made me good or bad. It's just a fantastic tool I can use to buy a kid a bike when they are sad or invest in my business so I can do more cool things. We can take our family on trips to have priceless experiences. Money is awesome, and it's everywhere. I'm just glad we finally have a good relationship. Abundance is your faith that there is plenty. But what if you lack resources?

I can't do it because:

lack of money, time, contacts, a better boss, education, opportunity, and the list goes on. But is this really the issue?

Never did I believe I needed to go to college to do big things. If you go, great. If you don't, great.

I didn't wait to have the perfected skill set or education before taking action toward my goals. I also didn't wait until I had all the money I needed or influence to open doors. I would proceed as if I had it all. It's all coming, and it always has.

How many people do you know who have convinced themselves that it takes resources before a dream can get started?

. . .

I'm here to tell you it has nothing to do with resources and everything to do with resourcefulness.

I don't have a Master's degree, but I have spent well over 150K on education.

I've been a part of growing a multimillion-dollar business, drove the fancy car, big house, and designer lifestyle. I willingly walked away to follow a dream without every piece figured out. I am building an empire.

I married a man completely the opposite of me, struggled tremendously, and then created a marriage I did not think possible.

I survived my daughter having multiple brain surgeries by the age of 3 and having my second daughter in the middle of it all.

I have been in the lowest points of depression, healed my body, and helped others do the same.

I have traveled throughout the country and world.

New Mexico hunting trips sleeping under a canopy of stars.

Dining top dollar in the Hamptons.

Book touring in Times Square

Shaking hands with the Pope in the Vatican

Teaching the newest hair trends in London.

And the list goes on.

I only tell you this because everything on that list was a dream that I got to check off my list. Now I have new dreams and new lists, and this book is a beautiful part of it all. I want you to see the power of having a dream and not giving up.

If we do this life right, we will never stop dreaming, and each dream realized is another depth of fulfillment. Fulfillment is true happiness. We must be growing to be fulfilled.

That's the power of being human. You are enough. There is enough. Abundance will make you so rich.

"Abundance is not something we acquire. It's something we tune into." -*Wayne Dyer*

PEP TALK

Here's the deal, yo... You want more out of your life; you have to get into flow with joy. But, I can't be happy until I get money, the house, the car, or the job you say. Friend, I'm here to tell you it has nothing to do with your want and everything to do with your attitude and flow. The desire is essential. Probably as much as the action steps to get started. But, just know if you forget the gratefulness aspect in the process, you are screwed. Gratitude keeps us in alignment and on track with true purpose. If you forgot gratitude today, take a minute to explore below.

EXERCISE

- Make a list of all that you are grateful for.
- How can you practice abundance in your own life?

CHAPTER 9

PEOPLE.
PEOPLE.
PEOPLE.
GOD LOVES
PEOPLE.

IF YOU LOOK
FOR THE BEST
IN PEOPLE,
YOU'LL LOVE
PEOPLE WHEN
THEY DON'T
SOUND LIKE
YOU, LOOK LIKE
YOU, OR SEE
EVERYTHING
LIKE YOU DO.

- Anna Ennis

9. PEOPLE. PEOPLE. PEOPLE. GOD LOVES PEOPLE

I CHOOSE TO SURROUND MYSELF WITH ALL WALKS OF life. I surround myself with homeless people, addicts, criminals, top-level entrepreneurs, millionaires, billionaires, adventure seekers, priests, preachers, yogis, shamans, my wild, crazy friends, and family. I'm a stranger to no one. I love people. I believe connecting with all walks of life has always helped me understand people. I love people just about as much as I love breathing air in and out. If you ask me where I have learned the most, it's from people. Watching, listening, asking questions, connecting, and caring to know more. My Dad gave me this gift.

He lived with a severe addiction to alcohol and, on the darkest occasions, drugs.

I remember being eight years old, driving home because my dad was too drunk to drive us. I was tall for my age, so I could reach the pedals and see over the steering wheel, but it didn't make me less afraid. I experienced countless times where my Dad's addiction spilled into my hands and left me angry and heartbroken. I wanted so badly to understand how he could choose substances over everything else that was important, be gone for so long, and not choose my brother and I over the life he lived. I saw up close the destruction that comes with addiction, and it repelled me, but I loved my Dad so much. I had to find another way to be close to him in my heart because the alternative was to hate him. I refused. I forgave him to set us both free. I chose not to judge him. I only wanted to love him, so that's what I did. I had healthy boundaries, but I looked for his big heart under his pain.

I appreciated anything that I could find that was positive, like his desire to give and help with anything he could manage. I stopped looking at all of our differences. I discovered how we were the same in so many ways. When his addiction took his life, I sobbed and grieved for some time. My faith increased more in this time than I ever expected. It was out of love for people that created a closeness then and now to each other. Although he is no longer here, I am reminded so often through my interactions with others. He taught me to look for the best in people and love in a way that I didn't know I could. He helped me not be afraid of people when we don't sound alike, look-alike, or see everything the same.

I find so much joy in connecting with people. I can say with certainty that my relationships with others are the single greatest asset that has kept me going when I've wanted to quit and cheered me on to my most significant achievements.

Connecting with others has expanded my world in some of the most exciting ways.

When I was 22, the day before Thanksgiving, I came home for a few days for the holiday. I had gone grocery shopping with my mom when the call came in that I would get the opportunity to train to be a business coach with some of the most elite business owners in our country. I would travel back east to Connecticut every six weeks for the next two years and learn from the best to help others with their businesses. This was a program I had dreamed of getting to be a part of but knew it was probably damn near impossible because of the criteria required. The time off work and travel alone were daunting, but suddenly, all those unknown factors didn't matter. I was chosen! Scared, intimidated-- totally out of my league felt like an understatement. I was damn near petrified.

. . .

This was quite the dream for a small-town girl who always had the heart of an entrepreneur. I remember jumping on a plane and not even being able to rent a car because the legal age was 25. Further, I had to take an hour-long taxi ride at midnight each time to get to and from my destination.

The next two years shaped my mind for business more than I can even explain. Not to mention my maturity. When you're surrounded by people who have achieved some pretty big dreams, you tend to set even bigger ones for yourself. Some of the people in the group were almost twice my age, millionaires, owned multiple businesses, and had garnered more success than I could fathom yet. What struck me most was how they all treated me. They treated me as their equal. Although I had been comfortable around diversity of all kinds, some part of me wasn't sure if I would be intimidated by such successful people. It forced me to think, look, and behave at my highest ability. I grew by light years with every trip.

I share this because who you're influenced by plays an enormous role in what you believe is possible for you to achieve. I had always dreamed more oversized than I knew what to do with, but it wasn't until this time in my life that I had learned they could come true. I saw people living out my goals. Ceilings blew off for me, and I knew the sky was the limit.

It was not the first time I had put myself in unfamiliar territory, but it was the furthest I had ever been from my comfort zone. To this day, 20 years later, I still have relationships with the majority of that group. The best part-- they still cheer me on. Relationships are everything.

I won't let myself be the smartest person in the room. I put myself in places with people who I may have no reason being around because of their education, success, or mindset feeling just beyond reach. That's where you grow...when you level up with the best. When you choose to put yourself out there when you know you don't quite belong yet, then you are nearly there.

It's now become this fun game where I see how uncomfortable I can get with people. I love to grow, and it keeps me going. Sometimes I need humbling and gratitude, so I serve. My mind is always expanded when I lay all I've got on the table with someone I have never met. Other times I need confidence and growth, so I surround myself with someone who knows so much more than me. At the end of the day, both experiences are powerful beyond words and bring me back to center. I've come to believe that we are made perfectly in the eyes of our Creator and that we need nothing. People and experiences are the elixirs to unlock our greatness. Without our experiences, we can't fully live into our potential.

An essential part of learning about yourself is knowing where you fall short and finding that missing piece in those we surround ourselves with.

I always laugh at the line from that movie Tobi McGuire of "You complete me," but it rings so much truth. Whether it's your partner in business, your best friend, or your husband or wife, it's crucial to attract that person into your life that seems the least suitable because of just how different they are from you.

Being your best self means being willing to have healthy opposition in your world to keep you grounded. When I choose relationships or leadership teams, I choose diversity, resistance, wild opinions, and opposing strengths not only for me but from each other.

. . .

The key is to bring a group of wildly different people together and teach them ways in which to respect each other right out of the gate. You don't always have to agree or like each other, but you do have to respect each other to move the needle. The most successful people I know are masters at this. I have learned it's not the easiest thing to do, but it's the best thing to grow at rapid speeds.

"My great blessing is my son, but I have daughters. I have white ones and Black ones and fat ones and thin ones and pretty ones and plain. I have gay ones and straight. I have daughters. I have Asian ones, I have Jewish ones, I have Muslim ones." - Maya Angelo

PEOPLE MATTER MOST!

PEP TALK

Sometimes it is not pretty, but we have to examine the relationships in our lives. Lean way into the discomfort of feeling out of place. Ask a lot of questions of yourself, especially the questions of who I spend the most time with? Take just a few minutes and contemplate the thoughts below. It will make a considerable difference to evaluate your life's relationships and whether they are giving to your soul or sucking the life out of you. They may be the reason your dreams may or may not be happening. Keep going. You got this.

EXERCISE

- What relationships have grown you the most, and why?
- What group or person could you meet with that could help you grow?
- Schedule a meeting with them, and don't be afraid to ask a lot of questions.

CHAPTER 10

SERIOUSLY. KEEP GOING!

THE WINS ARE
ALL WORTH THE
HITS YOU TAKE
WHILE PLAYING
THE GAME.
IF YOU GIVE UP
AT ANY POINT,
YOU WILL
NEVER MAKE IT
TO FREEDOM.

- Anna Ennis

10. SERIOUSLY. KEEP GOING!

I GREW UP IN JAMESTOWN. PART OF MY LIFE WAS IN A neighborhood where I could walk to school, and the greater part of my life was on a ranch. My husband teases me about my childhood being a little more like the Little House on the Prairie. We didn't have a TV most years of my life. My house was surrounded by land, cows, and mosquitos the size of flies. I spent my adolescent years not the least bit interested in being a part of the ranching life, but funnily all my coolest memories are filled with those who loved it all (except maybe the mosquitos).

Although I could appreciate the country lifestyle, I always saw myself at a quicker pace with more diversity. City-ish.

My inner entrepreneur first appeared at a very young age, but if you're asking for the most lucrative memory, it was this one. It started with a dare and ended with a few grand in my pocket. In high school, I was dared to join FFA (it had to happen through a dare because I knew nothing about being a Future Farmer of America). The dare included me raising animals for the county fair. I also knew there was a cash prize. I totally took it on.

My girlfriends wrote down different animals, and I drew from a hat. Guess who got turkeys? This girl right here. I would not back down from a challenge, and I wouldn't do less than my best. Honestly, I was determined to kick ass at raising these darn birds.

Boy did I raise turkeys. I wore the white official outfit, learned how to show, and entered our county fair. Hilarious that I even made it that far.

I took home 5 ribbons for three birds entered and a few thousand dollars cash in my pocket.

Folks, I knew then I was an entrepreneur. I'm not sure if I knew the word entrepreneur yet, but I knew I would write my own paychecks and do crazy things. Did I mention I had to butcher the turkeys myself? That's commitment.

I've packed in more life than I would have thought I could handle in the last 38 years. The wins have all been worth the hits I've taken while playing the game. If I had given up at any point, I would have never made it to the freedom I have today in life and business.

Of all the accomplishments that I have today, the one that stands out the most, possibly because it challenged and grew me the most, is my marriage to my husband, Jason. I'd like to sound all sappy and good wife-ish, but I think that would be a lie. I think people say marriage is challenging, but you have no clue until you are in the cuts of it. It turns out he's the best friend I've ever had and the person who has my back through feast and famine. I'm crazy about him today, and we're nearly a decade and a half into what we've built as a family. I can tell you for a fact there were points in our relationship that I've never wanted to quit anything more than I wanted to quit us. I did not always want to keep going. I'm not a believer in sticking out your marriage just for the sake of sticking out your marriage. I mentioned before I'm not a martyr, and there are no prizes for staying in something that makes you shrink. Jason, however, has always challenged me to be better and grow. This has sometimes looked like years straight of being pissed at each other without reprieve. This has looked like one of us being right and the other being dead ass wrong and still going to sleep in the same bed. We have always come out stronger and more in love in the end. I should plug counseling here. It works when you want to work for it, and we have fought for every square inch of happiness we have today. No one makes me laugh more than Jason. We are complete opposites, and sometimes I think we are a damn miracle. It brings me profound joy that we kept going. This morning, driving home from the gym, I was thinking of this book, and this cheesy thing came to my mind...Oh my God, I love Jason way more today than I ever did when we met. Thank God for grace because I would have been screwed at day one of this relationship without it.

How Jason and I met is a fun story. I was 25 and shopping on Christmas Eve for my brother at a Sports store on my way to our family cabin. I had sped into the parking lot, parked in the last front row parking spot, and ran into the store. Being consumed with the task of finding a last-minute gift, I didn't notice I had cut someone off who had been pulling into the prime real estate I'd parked in. He had politely entered the store and began shopping...which was far more mature than I. If tables were turned, I would have given him the stink eye and written him off as rude. I grabbed a gift, ran back out, and jumped in my car. To my surprise, I've got a note on my windshield. It read, "Would love to go out sometime." Jason.

What the hell was this? I thought my friend thinks he's so funny. This guy always has to be the funny one. So I call who I think is my old college buddy, Jason, to have a good laugh at his prank note. You know where this is going, it wasn't my old friend. This new Jason caught me off guard, and from sheer embarrassment, I said yes to a blind date because I never even saw him in the store.

All these years later and we are not just married but happily. Most days, I ask myself why in the heck does he put up with me. He's kind. Level headed. Empathetic beyond words. He's the rock to our family. I mean, I'm kind too, and I put up with him also, but he is so different from me in so many ways. I'm the "get up and dust it off!" one between us, and occasionally, I may or may not lose my shit.

If I'm honest, our first ten years were oil and water and fire and gasoline on really bad days. We said to each other on our wedding day that we would not get divorced unless someone cheated. That was the only deal-breaker. I gotta tell ya, there were days where we both regretted not adding to our list of "deal breakers," for example, if the sound of the other breathing has become too much, haha! Seriously though, we fought hard for our marriage. I think God was like, "ya, these two aren't giving up; let's give em' a break for a while."

I share this with you because there are moments that we all go through of intensity with our relationships; intimate, family, or friendships. Our business relationships and partnerships are included in this. For many of us, strained relationships are the jugular. We can have every single thing we've ever wanted to achieve but if the relationships in our lives are a wreck, everything feels rocked. It can REALLY make you want to give up. I have chosen my career and success over people many times in my life without meaning to. I've learned the hard way that it's all connected even when you don't want it to be. I've fed my ego for accomplishments that did nothing for my sense of purpose.

Our purposes always involve other people. There's not one person out there that has a purpose that doesn't involve another. We don't live in a vacuum. If you are feeling lost and wanting to quit personally or professionally, spend time enriching and strengthening your relationships. Your purpose will always show itself, and everything else will get back on track.

Let your dreams be your compass. Dreams give us life. So although we are in this time in our lives where it feels completely uncertain, we must dream, achieve, and keep going no matter what. It is not for significance or to please another but because how you show up paves the way, giving others permission to do the same for their lives.

Learn the instrument

Take the trip

Start the business

Learn a language

Adopt a child

Volunteer and give back

Teach someone something you know

Make the call to the family member

Go for the walk

Try mediation

Pray for the first time

Bake something new

Do something, and keep going.

Showing up big for your life requires messy, imperfect action.

You must embrace when you first jump out and try the dream on there's a good chance you will not be perfect. If I'm frank, you will probably suck at it. If I have learned anything, it's that you must do it before you can see it.

"Some people want it to happen, some wish it would happen, others make it happen." -*Michael Jordan*

PEP TALK

Remember uncertainty doesn't mean you stop. It means you take a minute to reflect, and then you get going again. Reset the goals and dreams you had. This means take a look at your current state and where you dream and adjust.
Keep going!

EXERCISE

- Action steps to a new space of living:
- Realign what makes you happy right now where you're at?
- Recreate from what was working to what can work.

EPILOGUE

My second favorite childhood icon.

> "If you can't fly, then run. If you can't run, then walk, if you can't walk, then crawl, but whatever you do, you have to keep moving forward."

> *-Martin Luther King JR.*

Sharing this book has been a dream of mine. If you made it to this last page and took away even one thing from this, I ask you for a 5-star review on amazon. This girl is on a mission just like you to be the best she can be. Plus, "best-selling" author just sounds more fun. I thank you, new friend, for being a part of my dream.

To all my friends, I say stay connected. You mean the world to me. I can't wait to get to know you better, share your story, life, and comment on mine...

Facebook @annaennis
Instagram @annaennis
YouTube @annaennis

If you are looking for more, there is always more from where this came from. Check out my website for the most current workshops, classes, courses, and speaking events.

Connect @ www.annaennis.co

Until next time,

Keep Going!

"Don't give up on your dreams when it's hard."

Love,

Anna

Made in USA - Kendallville, IN
1196195_9781950621187
11.18.2020 0736